FRONTISPIECE

The stile, illustrated on the cover and on the following page, was built during the reconstruction of a former carriage house foundation at our farm near Woodstock, Vermont. It allows easy access now to a terrace from which one looks across the rolling pastures and woodlands eastward to the distant hills of New Hampshire. The buried part of each step is roughly two-thirds the length of the entire stone and has been carefully weighted to provide stability and safety.

THE FORGOTTEN ART OF
BUILDING A STONE WALL

Practical Ways of How to Build A Tailored
Stone Wall Without The Use of Mortar

THE FORGOTTEN ART OF
BUILDING A STONE WALL

An Illustrated Guide to Dry Wall Construction

by CURTIS P. FIELDS

former Executive Director
Yale University Alumni Fund Association
and
former President of the
Woodstock (Vt.) Historical Society

Published MCMLXXI by
YANKEE, INC.
Dublin, New Hampshire

This Book Has Been Prepared by The Staff of
YANKEE, INC.
edited by
Richard M. Bacon
designed and produced by
Carl Kirkpatrick

•

illustrated by
Curtis Fields, Jr.

8th Printing

FIRST EDITION
Copyright 1971, by Yankee, Inc.

Library of Congress Catalog Card No. 78-169930

ISBN 0-911658-52-1

DEDICATION

To my wife, Betty, who shares my passion for stones and has become an expert at placing rollers.

CONTENTS

Editor's Preface

A modest, gentle man in his eighty-second year, Curtis P. Fields is well aware that few people have spent a large part of their leisure time building stone walls. For thirty years he has balanced the demands of an active life committed to various problems such as raising money for higher education with an enduring passion for working with stone. Now he can look about his Vermont homestead — interlaced, perhaps, with more stone walls than a man has need of — and take genuine satisfaction in his years of work and enjoyment.

Mr. Fields was asked to write this book and share his experiences as the result of an article about him by Larry Willard which appeared in YANKEE in October 1965.

His are not the common rubble walls of our forefathers that snake their way among the New England hills and through the trackless woodlands. They are fitted, patiently laid structures running ruler-straight and level, each stone bonded to its neighbor and laid with precision and love.

How many men can look about them and find such sure proof of their existence in something they have done with their own hands? In these walls there is solidity and strength and an imperviousness to Nature's force. Perhaps they will be standing — even and straight — long after we have vanished and are forgotten.

—◦✦◦—

FOREWORD

The Author at work.

From the first time I saw them in 1938, the two miles of neglected stone walls on our Vermont farm have excited and challenged me.

These included the poorly laid boundary walls surrounding our two-hundred acre property on Hartland Hill as well as walls lining both sides of the town road that bisects it. Additional stonework, often six feet high, had served as foundations of both the long-ago-burned barn adjacent to the house and of a smaller barn across the road which had met a similar fate.

Evidently most of these walls had been made simply by piling the stones helter-skelter primarily to clear land urgently needed for cultivation and pasture. Through the years many of them had been supplemented by two or three strands of barbed wire to keep cattle from escaping.

My interest in stone structures and rock formations was first aroused in 1910. However, it was slow to mature and stonework on our newly purchased property, which we soon came to call Penny Wise, had to be postponed until we could make the house itself livable. Then I began the pursuit of what was to become the most interesting, most engrossing, and most healthy pastime I have ever experienced.

Toward the end of the third year of working my way through DePauw University in Indiana as secretary to its President, I had the rare good fortune to be snatched away by Dr. John R. Mott, the General Secretary of the International Committee of Y.M.C.A.'s, who — on three days' acquaintance — invited me to travel here and abroad with him as his secretary. The President agreed with hearty congratulations and "sent me on my way rejoicing".

The callow youth, who scarcely remembered having noticed a stone wall during his twenty years of living in five different relatively flat Midwestern states, was due for startling awakenings.

During our first foreign trip I was increasingly fascinated by stone structures. In Cairo one man of our party (much older than I) challenged me to a race up the Pyramid of Cheops (the "Great Pyramid"). Its stone cubes are so massive and steep that all the way up one Arab boy had to pull me as another pushed from behind. While standing on the top, resting victoriously from the four-hundred-foot climb and drinking in the magnificent view in all directions (including that of the nearby Sphinx), I saw a third boy scampering up in our direction. To my amazement he handed me my friend's business card on which he had written that he must return because his heart was acting up. Since then I have often wondered how many in the past could have received a special-delivery message under similar circumstances.

Five thousand years ago, we are told, this pyramid had been built of some 6,000,000 tons of stone quarried along the east bank of the Nile, floated across in flood time, and dragged up a stone ramp that took ten years to construct. Herodotus reports that 100,000 men worked twenty years to finish the pyramid.

Another impressive stone monument greeted us when our party stopped not long after at Baalbek, Syria. Historians tell us that the original entrance to the now-ruined Great Temple consisted

Inclined planes of this type have been used in building stone structures in the Middle East for probably 5000 years.

of fifty-four stone columns eighty-eight feet high and twenty-two feet in circumference. Only six small columns were still standing.

Several years later I had the privilege of examining closely other noble examples of stonework: the Parthenon of Athens, the Santa Sofia Mosque of Constantinople (described as one of the two most beautiful buildings in the world), and still later, the fascinating ruins of the Roman Forum — in addition to many others nearer home.

In 1934 my dormant interest in how to use an individual stone matured suddenly while my wife and I were visiting her schoolmate in Center Conway, New Hampshire. Our hostess remarked that she and her children planned to call on a nearby farming family, the Littlefields. Would we like to go along and see their spectacular view of the mountains? Of course we agreed.

I found Mr. Littlefield behind the barn. He was seated on a granite ledge, drilling by hand a series of holes preparatory to splitting off a large slab.

After brief introductory remarks and comments on the weather and the view, the following taciturn conversation ensued:

"Would you mind if I watched you for a while?"

"No."

And later, "Would you be willing to show me how to do that?"

"Yes."

So I took his seat on the giant stone and picked up his tools. That was the beginning. It launched an involvment with stonework that has engrossed me for more than thirty years.

Shortly after the incident we left that granite area of New Hampshire and returned to Connecticut and to several years of a week-day round of commuting to New York.

In 1937 we moved from a rented cottage in the hills some five miles north of Greenwich to a house we had built on a three-acre hillside plot a mile or so nearer town.

We soon realized our urgent need for more level space around the house. That, of course, meant building retaining walls. We hunted up a Czechoslovak named Paul Chutka who had been highly recommended as a stone mason. He turned out to be short, stocky, good-natured, and a wizard at his job.

I seem to have been born with an urge to do things — constructive things — with my hands. So naturally I offered to help him when not too busy with the inescapable and considerably less interesting chores of thinning out elm trees, battling poison ivy, and cleaning up the debris left behind by the builders of the winding driveway up to the house.

Paul was soon wrestling with half-buried boulders — large and small — as he had been doing for many years around his own place several miles distant. Together he and I dug out many of these to the accompaniment of his cheerful "she coom, she gotta coom", and "coom" they soon did. Before long I found myself applying to the larger boulders the almost-forgotten rock-splitting routine I had learned behind the Littlefield barn.

And I was to continue these techniques the following year when we were fortunate enough to purchase our property in Vermont.

My wife had spent most of her life in and around Woodstock. I first saw that soul-satisfying spot in 1919 shortly after I was discharged from our flying corps, and we were married there eighteen months later.

It was while visiting in that village in 1938 that we learned by chance from a friend that a hillside farm four miles distant and seven hundred feet higher — with its pinnacle three hundred feet higher yet — had just come onto the market. Three or four days later we bought it at what proved eventually to have been a very modest price. The owner, a young man living there alone after his mother died, decided when his last barn burned that this latest tragedy was 'just one raisin too many' and was glad to move out.

Several considerations helped to clinch the matter for us: the attractive lines of the 1830 Greek Revival house, the rugged countryside with appealing views in all four directions, the miles of tumbled-down stone walls which bordered the farm and lined both sides of the rambling town road.

Some care — though by no means enough — had been used in laying the foundation of the 110-foot former cattle and hay barn near the house as well as those of the other farm structures.

My fingers itched to get at the stones we saw from our windows. But there was too much to be done with the house itself; a new roof was constructed, several dividing walls removed, one new one built, a fireplace and chimney installed, damaged floors replaced, the cellar renovated, and a sadly dilapidated carriage house torn down.

But as soon as basic repairs and improvements permitted, we began to spend our vacations at Penny Wise.

Courtesy Clara Dupuis Boulex

Two early views (above and below) of the author's home, "Penny Wise." The barns and sheds have fallen since these photos were taken leaving hundreds of feet of neglected foundation walls throughout the area.

Courtesy Merrill H. Henderson

At every opportunity since then I have been actively engaged in stone wall construction on our property. I have learned that it is not brawn that is needed so much as a basic understanding of the laws of physics, an awareness of the need for safety, and a practical knowledge of building techniques that can be acquired with forethought and experience.

In the following pages I have outlined some of the construction methods I have used, and described some of my results with the hope that working with stone will provide as much pleasure to others as it has given to me. □□

PART 1

OBSERVATIONS ON SAFETY

Lawrence F. Willard

Before describing some practical aspects of stone wall building that has occupied so much of my time these past years, let me emphasize one basic consideration: *be careful at all times.*

I learned this lesson the hard way.

One day I walked over to the southwest corner of the old tumbled-down barnyard wall to see what — as a beginning — I could do about the ugly pile of random stones between it and the nearby house. I inadvertently stepped on a loose stone, lost my balance, and fell backwards. My shoulders took the worst of the shock; nevertheless, my head got quite a jar.

Then and there I resolved never to be so careless again.

When I was first beginning to feel the lure of flat stones, I found myself muttering:

> *Should ancient crocks*
> *Play 'round with rocks*
> *Without a doc's*
> *Expert advice?*

With this in mind I made an appointment with my doctor. After a thorough going-over he gave me an unqualified O.K., but added, "Take it easy at first until you get hardened up. When you get tired, *stop and rest for awhile.*"

As a matter of course through the intervening years I have had periodic check-ups and I have formed the following rules:

Don't attempt stonework on a wet day. Wait until the stones have dried thoroughly, for sure footing will help to avoid accidents.

Watch your footing at all times. When you are carrying or 'rolling' heavy stones, don't walk on sloping ground without watching your step. Look out for loose stones underfoot.

Keep fingers and toes 'out from under'. Any stone slab is potentially dangerous while you are in the process of moving it. Make sure you have seen to it that its near corners are safely propped up by other stones or wooden blocks before you investigate its underside with your hands or feet. Even then, it's much safer to use the curved end of your pinch bar to remove anything loose from under the slab.

Wear gloves. Special work gloves with a gritty surface to fingers and palms, can be purchased in any hardware store. Because working with stones is continually abrasive, these will protect your hands from minor cuts and discomfort. They will also insure a better grip when you are in the process of moving a stone.

Keep a supply of the proper tools within easy reach. When you need a tool, that need may be urgent. I keep mine in the back of my Jeep.

Don't attempt to carry stones that are too heavy for you. Instead, tip them up on end or side, straddle them, and roll them along between your legs. If you must lift, make your legs do the work instead of your back. If a stone is much too heavy, lay a 2″ x 8″ plank on level ground (or if the plank is not level, shore it up with wooden blocks until it is) and move the stone along with the help of rollers. (see page 31) Or hitch it to your Jeep with a log chain and drag it. Or juggle it onto your stone boat and hitch that to your Jeep.

When working with dynamite to dislodge partially hidden stones, seek expert advice. Blasting rocks can be a dangerous and terrifying experience for the amateur as I explain in the following chapter. While I appreciate the advice and good intentions of friends, I have learned to seek professional advice, for I want to know in advance as much as possible about the effects of dynamiting and the necessary precautions one must take to insure safety.

Above all, *take it easy.* Use common sense. I can well imagine most accidents that occur while working with stones are the result of rushing or carelessness, or "bulling a job through".

> *Don't trust a stone*
> *Unless you hone*
> *To sigh and groan*
> *In bed, alone,*
> *With broken bone.*

PART 2

FINDING AND WORKING WITH STONES

Lawrence F. Willard

In our area of Vermont we have an abundance of mica schist* to work with. Unfortunately my earliest attempt at wall building was coupled with an experience that could have been disastrous, but together they launched an interest that has continued to provide gratification and good exercise for more than thirty years.

While mowing the lawn one day I found myself 'fed up' with dodging a stone, the corner of which stuck up some eight or nine inches. Fetching a spade, I dug and dug *and* dug until I had uncovered a flat ledge of beautiful mica schist six feet long, thirty-five inches wide, and heaven only knew how deep. It was buried at an angle of some sixty degrees.

I made a line parallel to its face and four inches down. Then I drilled six 4″ holes (as taught by Mr. Littlefield) and inserted wedges and shims in each. The sledge hammer soon produced the beginnings of a straight crevice which the crowbar quickly widened.

---

*Mica: *A group of minerals which are distinguished by their perfect cleavage, causing them to split readily into thin flakes . . . having an average hardness of 2.5 and specific gravity of about 3. (note: this is about three times as heavy as water).*
Everyman's Encyclopedia

Schist: *Any metamorphic crystalline rock having a foliated structure and readily split into slabs or sheets.*
Webster's Collegiate Dictionary

Then I wrapped a log chain around the resulting slab. Hitched to the Jeep, the stone was soon coaxed out of its hole and onto the stone boat. With the Jeep's help it was dragged to a spot near the northwest door of the house. There — thanks to wooden rollers on planks — it was soon installed as a decorative and most welcome doorstep.

Patricia H. Whitcomb

An ample slab of mica schist which the author split from a ledge using hand tools, and moved to provide an imperishable doorstep.

The next day, using a wooden block as a fulcrum, I tried to budge the remainder of the ledge with my five-foot crowbar. But, as Paul would have said, "She no coom."

Before long a friend stopped by to watch. As he was leaving, he volunteered to see what he could do with dynamite on his return the next day.

After studying the situation for awhile, he and two helpers placed the dynamite on the center of the sloping ledge, with debris piled below to prevent its slipping off. Then they piled on almost everything nearby that was loose, including brush and short logs. As a final precaution they draped my heavy log chain on top.

The leader suggested that we open all the windows of the house. He added that it might be just as well if all of us took refuge behind a large maple tree some eighty feet distant, and not far from the south door of the house. We did so. Then he set off the charge by means of a long electric wire attached to a plunger.

As one of the men described it afterwards, "All hell bust loose."

The logs flew over the wall some forty feet to the north (the ledge having sloped in that direction). Odds and ends flew every which way. The log chain disappeared completely. While we were searching for it, one of the men — with typical unsmiling Vermont humor — remarked, "My honest opinion is it hasn't come down yet." The chain was finally located seventy feet away, across the road and down a southeast slope.

When the dust had settled, I was left with a liberal supply of workable mica schist which I eventually was able to use for many of my projects.

"All Hell bust loose!"

(Editor's Notes: *Methods of Locating Suitable Stone in Your Area*
   The kind of wall most favored both for its looks and for the ease with which it can be constructed consists of flat, angular stones. Rocks rounded by glacial action and erosion are used in many miles of stone walls throughout New England, but they are harder to handle and more difficult to level and keep in place. Flat stones, on the other hand, can be laid up with some degree of precision. A dry wall does not require the use of mortar which in northern climates cracks when it is subjected to a range of temperature and frost action.
   If the reader is not so fortunate as to have at hand a workable supply of stone, there are ways of locating one. Should he be forced to travel too far afield, it can be a time-consuming as well as an expensive hobby. If time, however, is the primary consideration and not the

cost, he could talk with a local sand and gravel dealer or locate the name of one in the Yellow Pages of the telephone book. Such dealers will deliver truckloads of stone and deposit it where you want it.

There is a more adventurous way of locating stone when time and the necessary equipment are available to the hobbyist. For example, maps of any particular area are issued upon request for a small fee by state geologists*. On such maps different sections are portrayed in color and subdivided to show the locations of various types of rocks and minerals found in that area.

On the Vermont section map five of the main groups are further subdivided and refer to the schists, highly metamorphized rocks which are named for their characteristic minerals. Some of the other metamorphic rocks are gneiss, phyllite, slate, marble, and quartz, although the latter two do not cleave well. Mica schist has a high proportion of quartz and mica. In these rocks the mica flakes are oriented with their flat planes running in one direction which gives the schist its peculiar foliation and causes it to split in relatively straight lines. Other kinds of schists — hornblende, chlorite, or quartz — may be found in your area and all of these lend themselves to wall building.

Other extremely common rocks available for this purpose are the jointed igneous and metamorphic rocks that one sees throughout the countryside and which are particularly noticeable along highway and railroad cuts. Jointing, which results in regular and angular fracturing due to earth processes of stress and cooling, has produced some excellent building stones. Although they may not be perfectly rectangular, these jointed rocks will bind together effectively in any stone structure.

One way to use a geologic map is to couple it with the purchase of an inexpensive paperback book on the elements of simple geology and thereby learn to identify rocks in your immediate area. With the book and quadrant map in hand, wander the byroads of your vicinity and study the makeup of the stone walls and outcroppings. If you begin to notice the predominance of a rock type particularly suitable for your purposes and within easy hauling radius, consult your map and pinpoint such finds to see if a consistent pattern begins to emerge.

---

*Mr. Fields has such a map entitled Geological Map and Structure Sections of the Woodstock Quadrangle, Vermont (*Bulletin # 29, Plate I, 1947-65, of the Vermont Geological Survey; Charles G. Doll, State Geologist*).

Patricia H. Whitcomb

Mica schist is characterized by its definite "grain," or foliation which makes splitting a relatively easy matter.

In this way one could come upon an available lode of good stones. Of course, locating a source of supply and securing it might present two different problems. How you approach the acquisition of the stones and their transportation is best left to your own discretion.

Sometimes, here in New England where stones have been quarried for several hundred years, one will run across an abandoned stone pit. Ask some of the natives if they can remember such a deserted quarry. If so, it may be possible to gather substantial quantities of small-sized stones that were cast aside by the quarriers intent on securing only the largest and most saleable pieces.

Whatever methods you use to locate suitable stones, part of the satisfaction of doing this kind of foraging comes from the excitement of watching your stone pile grow.   End of Editor's Notes)

How to Split Granite

Earlier I referred to a short visit in 1933 to Mr. Littlefield in Center Conway, New Hampshire, when he was preparing to split a large slab from a granite ledge. He was good enough to tell me how he planned to do so and to let me drill — under his guidance —

one of the required six holes each of which was four or five inches deep.

For this operation he used three tools: *First*, a special type of 'grinding' chisel some fifteen inches long. Its upper part was 3/4" square with a flattened top to provide a good striking surface. The bottom half narrowed to a grinding surface shaped like an arrowhead and was about 3/4" wide. *Second*, a three-pound hammer with an 11" handle and two pounding surfaces each about 1 3/4" in diameter. *Third*, a light metal rod perhaps 3/16" in diameter and six or seven inches long. Its bottom 1/2" was flattened and curved to one side. Its purpose was to flip out the dust in the hole resulting from the gradual erosion.

To begin the drilling process the chisel was grasped in one hand, held vertically over a marked spot, and repeatedly and sharply struck with the hammer held in the other hand. After each blow the chisel was turned clockwise about sixty degrees.

That was my last and only experience with granite splitting, but before we left Mr. Littlefield did explain that after he had finished the last hole he would insert in each: *two metal shims* which were narrow at the top but flaring outward to provide finger grips, and wide at the bottom. Between each pair of shims he would insert a *metal wedge* that was wide at the top and narrow at the bottom.

These are the three drilling tools (see page 60) plus a wedge and shims, a set of which is placed in each hole drilled.
Patricia H. Whitcomb

Then with the sledge hammer he would pound each of the wedges once in consecutive order from one end of the line to the other and continue to do so until a thin crevice began to appear and had widened sufficiently to permit their removal before they could fall in.

Next he would insert two heavier metal wedges at opposite ends of the fissure. A few blows with the sledge hammer would increase the gap and soon the immense leverage afforded by the five-foot crowbar would force the crevice wide open and split the rock.

This is the method I used early in 1939 to split off a slab weighing about seven hundred pounds from the enormous ledge of mica schist which I found almost completely covered with sod.

More About Splitting Mica Schist

Before long I learned by trial and error how to split smaller pieces of mica schist — say, 6" x 12" x 24" — *without drilling holes*. This was done by using two heavy hand hammers one of which was flattened on both faces and was used to pound. The other, which received the blows, was squared on one of its faces and beveled to a splitting edge on the other.

This beveled edge was moved back and forth along the grain of the stone which stood upright on its narrow 6" side and at right angles to the body. It was pounded in three positions: middle, near end, and far end — over and over until a crevice began to show. Then a few blows on the middle of the longest side finished the job.

Further experiments soon showed that much larger slabs of mica schist could be split with comparative ease by the following method:

1)   the slab is propped up vertically on one edge by the use of large wooden blocks or stones.

2)   a straight line parallel to the grain is marked to indicate where the split is desired.

3)   move a heavy sledge hammer back and forth along this line while another man pounds it with a second sledge — one blow at each spot following Mr. Littlefield's *repeated* consecutive order.

4)   when a crevice begins to show, the blade of an old discarded ax is tapped lightly into the middle of the crack.

5) when it is far enough in to stand alone, it is driven in with sledge hammer.

6) when the crevice has opened sufficiently, the pressure of a crowbar soon provides two beautiful flat slabs.

Patricia H. Whitcomb

Left: Pounding the bevel-edged hammer with the sledge concentrates the blow to points along the line of the intended split scratched on the stone. Right: The crack is then opened with a wedge and crowbar.

One of the many advantages of mica schist stones is that if they don't fit the space for which they are intended (for instance, in the front face of your wall) they can be trimmed fairly easily.

1) prop up the stone's edge to a convenient degree with the pinch bar and insert a couple of small stones under it to hold it.

2) hold the bevel-edged hammer in one hand at a downward angle of about thirty degrees, but vary it as needed.

3) beginning near the *bottom edge* of the stone, chip it off bit by bit by pounding the bevel-edged hammer with the two-faced hammer.

4) attack another section a little higher up.

5) as this chipping-off process nears the top edge, remove the stone's props.

6) square off the desired straight line by breaking off small bits

at a time while holding the hammer perpendicular to the stone.

Don't attempt to hurry the process; otherwise, you may break off larger pieces than you wish.

Remember the old saying, "The hurrieder I do, the behinder I get."

Patricia H. Whitcomb

The face of a stone is trimmed from bottom to top. Here the author holds the bevel-edged hammer (in his left hand) at the proper angle and strikes it with the three-pound hammer.

How to Handle Heavy Stones as the Wall Becomes Higher

I use various methods to move heavy stones into place when the wall is more than two or three feet high. Each amateur stone worker will doubtless develop others as he goes along.

Always first measure with a yardstick the three dimensions of the space to be filled and search for the slab that comes nearest to meeting these specifications. If it doesn't quite fit, it can usually be trimmed. Then

1 – rest one end of a 2" x 8" x 8' plank on the wall and the other end on the ground at right angles to the wall.

A) roll the slab up the plank, or

B) rest it flat against the plank and work it up end-over-end or side-over-side, or

C) instead of using a plank, lay against the wall a descending series of eighteen-inch blocks (e.g., 12" x 12", 8" x 8", and 4" x 4"), then

   a) tilt the stone up on its end or side

   b) straddle it

   c) roll it up onto one block after another (lifting with your right hand and guiding the stone with your left) until one corner is safely supported by the wall. Then,

   d) tip the stone and let it fall onto the wall.

Any one of these simple devices may help to save one's back while lifting numerous stones to the top of a wall.

OR, *2* – If the slab is 2½ to 3 feet long,

   A)   lay a second plank parallel to the first (with just enough space to walk between the two), tilt the slab until it rests on both planks, and proceed as in *1-B* above, or

   B)   push the planks together and work the stone up them by laterally moving one side five or six inches upward, then the other side, and so on until it can be maneuvered onto the wall.

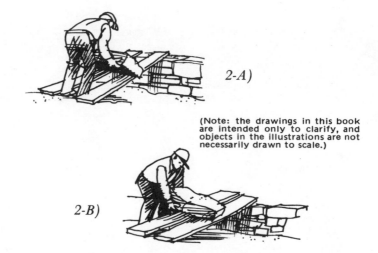

2-A)

(Note: the drawings in this book are intended only to clarify, and objects in the illustrations are not necessarily drawn to scale.)

2-B)

Longer slabs may be more easily lift-
ed in place by the use of two planks.

   3 – If the ground behind the wall slopes upward — but not too steeply —

   A)   load the slab onto the stone boat, hitched to a Jeep.

   B)   drag it to the most convenient spot behind the wall.

   C)   block up its downhill end sufficiently to insert two or three inches of a 2″ x 8″ plank (#1, below), with a roller between the stone and the plank.

   D)   with blocks, level off the downhill end of the plank, and

   E)   if a second (#2, below) is needed, insert two or three inches of #2 under the downhill end of #1 and level it.

F)   urge the stone along with a pinchbar.

G)   whenever a roller becomes free, move it along to a new spot nearer the wall.

4 – If the slab is too heavy for method *3,* the job can be accomplished without too much trouble if a four-foot plank is placed on the rollers on Plank #1 and the stone maneuvered onto it. The combination can then be pushed along with the pinch bar.

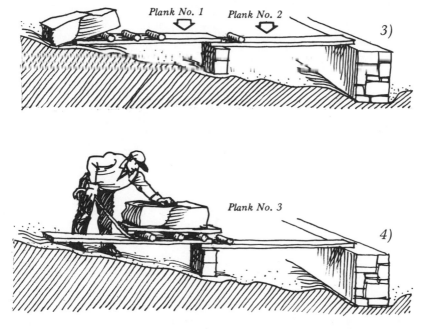

Rollers are essential in dealing with heavy stones. A short plank (No. 3) placed on rollers allows an even greater load. Keeping the planks level is important for safety.

When two or three sections of the wall have been entirely finished and are level, an alternative method is to place two planks end-to-end on the wall and with Plank #3 on rollers, as described in *4* above, a slab of almost any reasonable weight can be persuaded to ride to its final resting place on the wall.

You may now and then run across a beautiful flat stone in an old wall that is so large and so difficult to get at that, rather than use the stone boat, it will be much easier to use the Jeep alone.

To do so, this sequence is recommended:

1)   block up the front end of the slab six or seven inches and wrap a small log chain around it and hitch it to the Jeep; then pull it out on level ground.

The "hook and link" knot is quick and easy.

2)   block up each corner of that end a second time and maneuver the 'hook and link' knot until it is *under* the stone. This is a flattened hook at the end of a log chain designed to fit around any of the links in the chain quickly and easily. Pull the other end of the chain forward *between* the blocks.

3)   back the Jeep until it is practically over the end of the slab, hitch the chain as tightly as possible to the trailer hitch or to the framework of the Jeep, and remove the wooden blocks from under the stone. If the slab remains suspended on the end nearest the Jeep, its dragged end will smooth out a roadway rather than leave a scar.

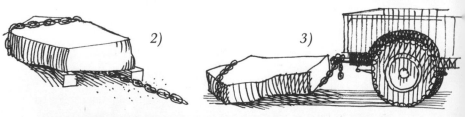

A large stone partially buried in an old wall may be more easily removed without a stone boat by using this method.

Last fall I needed to move a flat slab weighing about a ton down a gentle slope and onto a wall. A young grandson was visiting us at the time. Using a big crowbar, we blocked up the slab's four corners enough to allow easy working room. Under its nearest end we pushed about a foot of plank, placed a roller on it, and let the slab down onto the roller.

Following the same procedure as in *2* above, we wrapped the smaller log chain around the slab's farthest end, maneuvered the 'hook and link' knot into place, pulled the end of the chain out, up and over a sturdy, hollow metal cylinder and forward to the end of the plank. This cylinder — or any similarly shaped object such as a short log — that is some ten inches in diameter is placed across the slab. Then by attaching a heavy chain to the lighter one and pulling with the Jeep, we changed the direction of the thrust to a vertical one. Slowly and cautiously we dragged the captive slab to within a few inches of the chosen spot where — with the aid of the pinch bar — it was moved laterally into place.

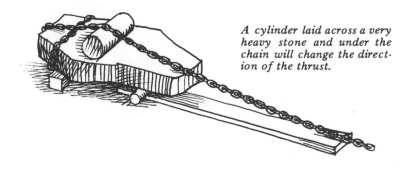

A cylinder laid across a very heavy stone and under the chain will change the direction of the thrust.

PART 3

BUILDING NEW STONE WALLS

Patricia H. Whitcomb

The planning and laying out of a new freestanding wall is perhaps the ultimate challenge to the builder. By its very nature this type of construction demands precision, for unlike the retaining wall — one side of which is banked with soil — the freestanding wall must be both solid and attractive from both sides. Whether it is a curved wall or one which runs in a straight line, the builder knows from the beginning that if the finished product is to be an addition to his landscape plan and an honor to his 'trade', he will have to pursue a strategic method of attack.

These are some of the steps which I have learned to take as I plan a new wall.

1) Locate and dig up or 'steal' from your tumbled-down walls a plentiful supply of mica schist stone which you segregate into convenient nearby piles roughly as follows:

   A) flat 1' x 2' x 2" to 4" thick stones, the largest and finest which should be reserved for the top of the wall.

   B) smaller sizes than the above, provided they are flat.

   C) random stones and pebbles that will be used to fill in interstices between the larger stones to keep the soil from seeping in and to prop up stones so that a level line can be maintained.

2) Chart the line of the wall, either straight or curved. Some people have the ability to do this by eye alone and having once established where they want the wall to be, they go ahead without further preparation. Others must rely on a guide line stretched between two stakes to provide a check for accuracy. If the stakes are as high as the proposed wall is to be, the taut line is raised upon the completion of each tier of stone and the evenness of the wall can be checked while it is under construction.

When plotting a curved wall it is sometimes a good idea to use a flexible garden hose to establish the foundation line of the wall. The hose can be shaped along the ground to simulate whatever curve is wanted. Landscape gardeners have used this device in laying out the curves of a flower bed. With an edger or shovel dig into the ground along the line of the hose and remove the turf. In this way the arc will serve as a guide in laying the first tier of stone. Beyond that you will have to depend on your eye for precision.

3) Excavate a section perhaps six feet long by some 40" wide and down to a depth that will provide a firm footing for the foundation stones. This depth will vary with the topography but it is important to be able to set the first tier solidly if the wall is to withstand the action of settling and heaving. The width of the excavation will provide plenty of room for your feet as you set the lower tiers, but be sure you have shoveled the loose soil out of the way to avoid the danger of tripping over it.

4) Provide proper drainage for the first tier of stones by

   A) choosing flat stones of irregular shapes, leaving an inch or so of space between them, and filling such spaces with small stones from your random pile. Crushed quartz is excellent for this purpose. After the foundation has been laid, one should allow the stones in later tiers to touch their neighbors.

   B) laying flat stones over the interstices to prevent seepage of soil.

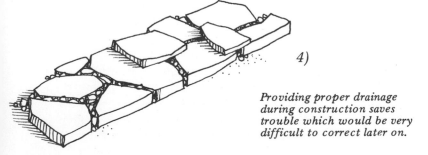

4)

Providing proper drainage during construction saves trouble which would be very difficult to correct later on.

5) Because a freestanding wall demands precision of construction on both faces of the wall, be sure to lay the front and rear stones so that in each case they follow a straight line. A folk saying in connection with non-tailored walls that might bear repeating during this phase of the construction is always to lay a wall so that each stone casts a shadow. If this is done, one will build a vertically straight wall, not one that tapers as it gets higher.

6) An effective width from the front to the back of a wall is from 26″ to 30″. With the additional ten inches of footroom in the excavation, one should have enough freedom of action.

7) If any stone you lay is not level, shim it up with small, flat stones until it is.

8) Occasionally lay cross-stones from front to back to bind the whole mass together.

9) If you are building a wall along sloping land, *step* the top of the wall up or down a foot or so when needed to conform to the terrain and to avoid excessive and unnecessary heights. How often and how much of a step each time will depend upon the degree of slope and your judgment as to what looks best under the circumstances. The important thing from the point of view of *look*s when working with flat stones is to make sure that between such steps the wall is *level*.

10) In laying stones, remember this basic formula:

ONE OVER TWO — TWO OVER ONE

Adhere to this formula throughout construction for its ability to bind stones together. This is especially important at points of stress — step-ups (see photo at right) corners, wall ends, stiles, and steps.

Why This Continued Emphasis on Keeping Stones Level?

The most important reason is the obvious fact that gravity pulls rocks down. If a stone slab that is not level is resting on another sloping stone, this downward pull of gravity is correspondingly increased.

To prove my point try the following experiment:

Patricia H. Whitcomb

This wall conforms to the slope of the land with a step-up and its strength is based on each stone being level, touching every stone around it, and fitting into the one-over-two, two-over-one pattern.

Place a flat slab weighing 100 to 300 pounds on a hard, level base and notice how difficult it is to shift it laterally. Then bed the same stone on a hard, sloping surface and observe how comparatively easy it will be (using a pinch bar) to persuade it to slide downward, inch by inch.

Winter's alternating freezings and thawings accentuate to a marked degree this tendency of un-level stones to slip downward.

A quotation from *Everyman's Encyclopedia* is enlightening: "On freezing, water expands by 1/12 its bulk . . . One cubic foot of water weighs 62.428 pounds . . . In the act of freezing, ice undergoes a noteworthy expansion so that ice at zero centigrade is not so dense as water as is proved by the fact that it floats thereon."

On the other hand, a flat stone slab resting on a level bed and supported by other flat stones, merely rises in freezing weather and, when the ice melts, settles back with no perceptible lateral movement.

This problem is a serious one in much of New England with its untold miles of old, weatherbeaten, loosely piled stone walls. Recall Robert Frost's poem, "Mending Wall":

> *"Something there is that doesn't love a wall,*
> *That sends the frozen-ground-swell under it,*
> *And spills the upper boulders in the sun;*
> *And makes gaps even two can pass abreast."*

Patricia H. Whitcomb

Walls built without attention given to leveling, drainage and binding often disintegrate as a result of winter's freezing and thawing.

In the face of this evidence it was startling to read several years ago an article by a man claiming to have discovered a 'secret' method of construction — namely, two outside layers of *inward sloping* stones between which random stones were simply piled on top of each other (with no evident effort made to bind them to the outside layers or to each other).

In one ten-hour working day, the writer added, he had 'constructed' such a wall fifty-one feet long, two feet wide, and three feet high, while his 17-year-old son collected the random stones and brought them to the construction site in a wheelbarrow.

Just imagine what would happen sooner or later to such a wall built on a sloping Vermont hillside! In the course of forty-eight hours I have seen the thermometer outside a north window of our Vermont village house where we live in the winter change seventy-two degrees.

Of course more rubble walls than flat, tailored walls do exist throughout New England. Within the memory of living men these were constructed at the rate of fifty cents a rod. But if one is to build them, he must be prepared to play Robert Frost's "kind of outdoor game" and spend time each spring picking up the loosened stones and wearing his fingers "rough with handling them".

This Brings Us Once More to the Question of Drainage

When a wall is finished, great care should be taken to see that at least a moderate slope of sod is provided both in front of it and behind it to drain away rain and melted snow and ice.

If the ground behind the wall is a hillside with more than a

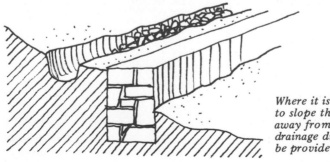

Where it is impossible to slope the ground away from a wall, a drainage ditch should be provided.

moderate degree of slope, a 'carry off' drain, several feet wide, should be excavated and perhaps filled with crushed stone. Its depth will depend upon the steepness of the hillside slope and the greatest depth of snow that accumulates upon it in any winter.

Remember that a gentle spring freshet in this part of New England may suddenly — though briefly — turn into a destructive torrent. Ask any Vermont road commissioner!

Curved Walls

Shortly after buying our farm I uncovered an immovable ledge sloping downward toward the northwest. It proved to have a beautiful flat end-face about eight feet from an existing wall.

Since the land slopes from west to east, the only solution for using this ledge seemed to be to construct a curving wall the top of which would be level all the way with the top of the end-face of the ledge. The new wall now curves westward to the point where it meets rising ground and eastward to where it joins the barnyard wall.

The resulting grass plot in front of the wall is now a very pleasant sight as we view it from the east porch or a north window.

Patricia H. Whitcomb

The author took advantage of a natural outcropping of ledge too large to move by incorporating it into a curved wall.

Patricia H. Whitcomb

These walls curve back to join the upward slope of the ground. They are separated by about five feet of level lawn.

That was one of the first curved walls which I constructed.

Later, about thirty feet west of the house, we worked on an unsightly passageway cut into the hillside. Lined with the usual roughly laid walls, it sloped slightly upward to a larger area (similarly walled) which obviously had once been the site of the first of two end-to-end farm structures of the style sometimes nicknamed "Vermont Continuous". This area had gradually been filled with mounds of miscellaneous rubbish. As soon as I could find time, I carted this mess — load after load — to the town dump.

Then I rebuilt the first 24 feet of the north and south passage walls, joined them with a nine-foot west wall, and finished off the latter with a semicircular recess set into its top. This presently houses a small fountain which overflows into an outward-flaring semicircular basin at ground level. Sufficient soil was then carted in to even off the empty space behind.

The next problem was that of constructing two curved retaining walls that would hold back a higher level of soil. They are essentially easier to build than a freestanding wall for only their facing sides must be fitted with precision. One was to run southwest to meet that slope and the other to curve northeast to meet an eastern slope.

Four right-angled corners had to be bonded carefully — two at the east end of the passageway and two at its west end. And, of course, step-by-step all along the course of these curved uphill walls each individual stone in each layer had to be shimmed up level before adding the next tier.

It soon became obvious that if all this stone work ended up at the same height the finished job might look like a fortress. The answer was a second set of curved walls parallel to the first, and some five feet distant with sod between them.

Once the bottom layer of stones had been leveled off and bonded to its neighbors, the task was simply a problem of following normal wall-building procedure at each step.

The final result has proved eminently satisfactory to live with and has given us pleasure ever since.

Patricia H. Whitcomb

The author's solution to the problem of an unsightly foundation included terracing to avoid a massive appearance at the front. A fountain at the back overflows into a basin at ground level.

How to Build a Right-Angled Corner

Through the years a weak corner of a freestanding or a retaining wall can have a devastating effect on the adjoining sections of a stone wall. Therefore, construction of right-angled corners require special care.

At the northwest corner of the barnyard were many examples of careless workmanship. Few stones were securely bonded to one another. Apparently little, if any, thought had been given to the urgent need of preventing seepage of water and loose soil. Behind both sections of the wall there was a rich harvest of stones of all sizes, many flat but most of them round — all simply piled on top of each other.

These piles, providing approaches from the west and north, were covered with a thick bank of sloping soil which in turn supported a generous sprinkling of flat stones.

When everything had been removed down to hardpan and after a proper sub-surface foundation for the wall had been prepared, work on the right-angled corners could begin.

I realized that to provide the necessary support each stone in

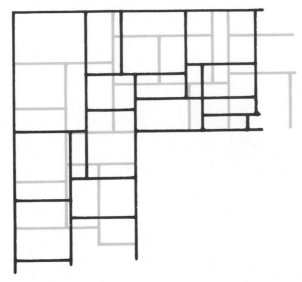

Each new layer (shown in black) should overlap the lower tier of stones (grey) both front-to-back and left-to-right to insure proper binding of a corner.

each tier had to be laid so as to bind most effectively those surrounding it as well as those above and below it. What a job of fitting and precision! But if one can accomplish it, the resulting corner should stand for a long time to come.

Patricia H. Whitcomb

A well-constructed corner in which the principles of levelling and overlapping stones have been observed.

Two Allied Problems

HOW TO CONSTRUCT THE END OF A FREESTANDING WALL AND
HOW TO PROVIDE AN OPENING FOR A GATE

The chief difference between these kinds of construction is only
one of degree: the end of the freestanding wall has but one face;
whereas, if somewhere along the course of the wall a gap is needed
for a gate, such a space requires two faces — one on each side.

In either case the individual stones of the face must not only
be bound to each other but — even more important — must be of
such sizes and laid in such a manner as to tie together the two
sides of the wall itself.

The end of the freestanding wall, without proper bonding of
its two sides, is subject to special dangers. Apart from the usual
hazards of winter's freezings and thawings, its individual stones
can often be accidentally dislodged by man and beast. Hence,
special care must be taken — tier by tier — to tie each stone together all the way from the sub-surface foundation to the top
of the wall.

Patricia H. Whitcomb

*At the end of a freestanding wall, or a passageway, cross-stones should
be placed the width of the wall to tie both sides together.*

Obviously, both faces of the gap for the gateway will need to be built in accordance with the same bonding and leveling principles. The distance left between the faces will depend on the use for which the gate is intended and the dimensions of the gate itself.

There are many types of gates: stretched wire stapled to upright posts and hinged by loops; custom-made wooden ones, using either

A simple type of gate may be made with wire and posts.

horizontal boards or pickets; and ready-made gates of wood or metal that can be purchased from most local building or farm supply houses.

The final decision as to which type is to be installed is determined by the dimensions of the space desired, its use, the conformation of the land, and the convenience of the user.

Another Usable Gap

When a freestanding wall is built at right angles to a pasture border — whether of stone, wood, or wire — another great convenience can be provided if a gap of about twelve inches is left between the end of the wall and the border. This will afford sidewise passage for the human body but will be impassable for horses and cattle. If the pasture border is barbed wire, the points should be bent down and driven into the wood of the post.

A Third Convenience

A further method of gaining access through a wall is the construction of steps leading from one level to another. The same

Patricia H. Whitcomb

*This gap of about twelve inches between the wall and fence post allows
a person through, but is narrow enough to restrain livestock.*

general building principles apply to the stone faces on either side of the opening. However, there are three additions or exceptions to consider:

1) each step slab in the series should be wide enough to provide sufficient foot-room, long enough to permit its being tied into both the right and left-hand faces of the gap, and thick enough to carry its own weight plus the weight of a man with any load he may have in his arms.

2) the steps should be buttressed with at least a modicum of stone foundation beneath.

3) for the sake of both safety and of good looks, there should be installed at ground level both above and below the series of steps, a slab about 20" wide and long enough to overlap the gap by at least 6" both to the right and to the left.

Patricia H. Whitcomb

Above: Wide slabs installed at both the top and bottom of a series of steps will increase safety as well as provide a tailored appearance.

Opp. page: A stone step must be long enough to be anchored into the wall securely at both ends. It must also be supported by smaller stones beneath it, and levelled.

Stiles

A TIME-HONORED BUT UNUSUAL CONVENIENCE

One seldom sees stone stiles set at right angles to a wall in our part of the country; at least, I haven't been conscious of them. They seem to be more common in older European farming communities than they are here. However, I have built a stile into each of three different walls near our house.

They are convenient, time saving, and attractive. They make it unnecessary to walk to the end of a wall and back again on the

Each step in the stile is set well into the wall during construction and worked into the one-over-two, two-over-one pattern.

opposite side to reach a particular spot. They add considerably to the general interest of the landscape. Guests enjoy using them; children adore them; and a stile makes a recurrent conversation piece.

They have disadvantages, however. Stiles have to be built with special care for safe and easy use. The tread must be adequate to accommodate a wide variety of users and to avoid the danger of stumbling. Since each step is laid at a right angle to the wall as it is being constructed, it must be anchored sufficiently well to assure permanence.

I have found that the best dimensions for each step seem to be about 15″ x 15″ and approximately three to four inches thick. The rise between the steps — from the top of one to the top of the next above it — should be perhaps 12″.

If these dimensions of the exposed part of the step are enough to bear the weight of various users, it follows that the buried part of each step should be the same thickness and depth from front to back but at least *twice as long*. Above it the wall-face stone (though at right angles to the half-buried step) should probably be just as long as the buried part of the step, for this will insure a permanent and immovable anchor.

Under no circumstances should one use as a stile step a mica schist stone which is found to have been buried in water-soaked ground for any length of time. Water-logged mica schist tends to retain water and to break if exposed to sufficient strain.

Although more difficult and challenging to build than the usual wooden-step stile which crosses over a wall, parallel to it, the stone stile assumes a permanent place in the construction of the wall and once installed, requires no maintenance.

PART 4

REBUILDING
OLD
WALLS

W hat should one do about the neglected foundation of a still-standing barn or shed?

My only suggestion is to seek the advice of a well-equipped and trusted contractor.

Most New England barns have low foundation walls 'below stairs'. Because of the lack of headroom, the removal and carting away of unusable rubble, the excessive amount of excavation involved to reset the wall and provide proper drainage (especially if the foundation has been built into the side of a sloping hill), and the hauling in and storage of needed flat stones would all prove a gargantuan task for the amateur.

But even if all that could be safely accomplished, and the layers constituting the first several feet of the wall constructed, the laying of the remaining stones might be a hopeless job.

The contractor with his various kinds of mechanical equipment can quickly do the necessary excavation and provide concrete walls of proper strength, lay perforated drainage pipes at the required depth, cover them with gravel, and top them off with soil.

All of this is expensive, but it will end your troubles.

How About Foundations of
Burned-Out or Razed Barns?

These are likely to present some difficult problems too — particularly if situated on a sloping hillside —but might be easier to cope with than if the building were standing. At least there is headroom. My advice, however, is to tear the walls down and start all over.

The barn at Penny Wise had burned before we purchased our farm, but it had been described to us as 'once one of the largest barns in the area'. The remaining foundations show that it measured 30 by 110 feet overall. Its foundations, as well as the cattle yard which ran along the south side of the barn on the house side, all consisted of stone walls five or more feet high. They had been laid with reasonable care but with little, if any, attention to the problems of drainage and of binding each flat stone to its neighbors.

The south side of the barn itself had once rested on wooden posts standing on large, flat stones.

Steeply sloping approaches on the west and north entries to the barn had been provided by loosely piled stones covered with soil. Through the years the freezing and thawing and inevitable pull of gravity had had a devastating effect. In one instance part of the foundations had been forced some fifteen degrees out of plumb.

This, of course, added a sporting flavor to the job of removing heavy flat slabs which now and then were found to be resting on others at downward-sloping angles. The woodchucks had industriously taken advantage of the resulting cavities and caused further havoc.

Once You Have Decided to
Replace a Wall, What Next?

Work on one six-to-eight-foot section of the wall at a time. This avoids an excessive amount of mess all at once and will give you a sense of accomplishment.

Remove all stones and soil down to a solid footing and excavate to a width from front to back of about four feet. This provides the necessary foot-room and will leave sufficient space behind the wall to be filled in later with random small stones and pebbles for drainage.

The next step is to sort all usable stones into piles such as mentioned on page 34 under *1. A, B, & C.*

Haul away all loose soil and useless stones so as to prevent overcrowding and the danger of stumbling.

If the compacted footing slopes in any direction as you lay the foundation stones, shim up each one with small flat stones until it is level. Then proceed to reconstruct the section according to previous suggestions before going on to dismantle and rebuild the next eight feet.

Below: Neglected walls provide ample material for rebuilding. The ravages of weather and woodchucks and the apparent lack of care taken in building this wall have resulted in its disarray.

Opp. page, top: Reconstructing a wall is begun by completely tearing down a six to eight foot section and clearing debris from underfoot.

Opp. page, bottom: The completion of each section provides contrast between the new and the old and gives further incentive to dismantle and rebuild the next section.

Resisting the temptation of using the largest slabs during construction pays off in appearance when the top of the wall is completed.

The Finale

What better way to end these thoughts on stone construction than with a brief discussion of the natural climax of the wall — its top.

If enough of the best and largest flat stones have been saved to top the wall (as suggested earlier) and if enough care has been taken to level each stone, the final tier is not only the culmination of the wall but constitutes the cohesive force which strengthens, supports, and binds together all its hidden parts in addition to protecting them from the ravages of winter's excesses.

Of course, to reserve such stones in the heat of construction is a challenge to one's self-discipline. If he has exercised control in this respect, however, he will find that a level, well-laid dry wall is a fine addition to the landscape.

Whether viewed from the side, from above, or from a distance against the background of a sloping forest or meadow, these walls will prove a source of increasing pleasure in all seasons through the years.

Though never as perfect as its amateur builder had hoped, he can derive continuing comfort from the thought, "A poor thing, but mine own!"   Patricia H. Whitcomb

"Penny Wise" today sits surrounded by walls the author has patiently re-constructed.

APPENDIX

WALL-BUILDING TOOLS AND EQUIPMENT

Patricia H. Whitcomb

Stone boat.

1. A Jeep, or similar vehicle with four-wheel drive and a low-low gear, fitted with a metal ball below the tail gate to which the trailer's tongue or stone boat's curved hook can be attached.

2. A trailer for hauling loose soil and small stones. Ours was made by a down-country town employee thirty years ago who often spent evenings 'moonlighting' on odd jobs. This ingenious man found an old Essex chassis, two usable wheels and tires to match — all in the town dump. To them he added a wooden bed, sides, and two hinged ends. He charged me only forty dollars, and although several years ago I had to replace the wooden floor, sides, and tongue we are still using it.

3. A stone boat for moving large stones. Buy the curved metal front piece at a farm equipment center and bolt to it three 2″ x 8″ x 6′ planks. Bind them together with a 2″ x 6″ at the rear. This, plus 2″ x 4″ x 6′ pieces on each side, will keep the stones from joggling off if the ground is rough.

4. An ordinary yardstick — needed at practically every step.

5. A sturdy wooden level that won't break if you drop it on a stone, and an unwarped 2″ x 6″ x 8′ plank to rest it on.

6. Two spades, one with a short and the other with a long handle.

7. A five-foot crowbar. Wasn't it Archimedes who said, in reference to the principle of the lever, "Give me where to stand and I will move the earth"? A shorter crowbar also comes in handy once in awhile but is not essential.

8. A pinch bar, sometimes called a wrecking bar, some 2′ long. One end curves in a wide arc with a notched nail puller. The

Patricia H. Whitcomb

Some of the tools that are necessary for wall building are (from left to right) a small bevel-edged hammer for trimming stones, a heavy sledge, metal wedges, a 25-pound bevel-edged hammer, a pinch bar, a combination mattox and pickax, and a five-foot crowbar.

Necessary for splitting rock by drilling are these hand tools: (top to bottom) hand drill or grinding chisel, three-pound hammer, a wedge and shims, and a stone-dust remover.

other is flattened and flares just enough to slip under the edge of a slab and provide powerful leverage. It is useful in shoving a slab forward or raising its edge a bit to permit the insertion of the tip of a crowbar. I find a second pinch bar is also helpful when both hands are needed to shift a stone laterally.

9. A combination mattock and pickax for rooting out stones that are partially buried. WARNING: Don't use the pointed end to pull out a slab without first making sure that the underside of the rock is flat or nearly so. I made that mistake once but never again! The point of the pickax slipped out suddenly because of the slope of the stone and threw me off balance. The answer is to drive the flat mattock under the stone, stand in front of it, and pull the handle until you are able to raise the stone and slip a wooden block under it. Then use the crowbar.

10. Four hammers: two double-faced, one a sledge weighing 15 pounds and one three pounds; two bevel-edged hammers, one 25 pounds and one about three pounds.

11. Two log chains, one heavy and the other light. Each will have a curved hook at one end to fit the metal ball on the Jeep; at the other end, a fold-back hook which will fit any convenient link when the chain is wrapped around a slab.

12. Half a dozen sets of small metal wedges and shims plus a stone-dust remover while drilling. These, in addition to two or three hand drills — one of which can be kept as a spare while the others are being sharpened — all can be purchased from or ordered by a hardware store. Electric stone drills are manufactured but their source of power sometimes makes them inconvenient and they do tend to be expensive for the amateur.

13. An old and discarded ax blade — no matter how rusty — for widening a crevice that is just beginning to show.

14. A supply of wooden or metal rollers a foot or two long and from 1" to 4" in diameter.

15. A liberal supply of wooden blocks about 2' long and anywhere from 2" x 2" to 8" x 10" in dimension; a half-dozen 2" x 4" x 6" blocks for shimming up heavy stones in a hurry; and several 2" x 8" planks to use when moving heavy stones to their positions in the wall.